LIFE LINES AND LESSONS

27 Lessons From the Journey of Life

SHAREE BENJAMIN-ROBINSON

Authored by Sharee Benjamin-Robinson

© Sharee Benjamin-Robinson 2025

Cover design Marcia M Publishing House

Edited by Lee Dickinson, Marcia M Publishing House editorial team.

All rights reserved 2025 Sharee Benjamin-Robinson

Sharee Benjamin-Robinson asserts the moral right to be identified as the author of this work. The opinions expressed in this published work are those of the author and do not reflect the opinions of Marcia M Publishing House or its editorial team.

Published by Marcia M Spence via Marcia M Publishing House, author services, West Bromwich UNITED KINGDOM, on behalf of Sharee Benjamin-Robinson. Email: info@marciampublishing.com

This book is sold subject to the conditions that it is not, by way of trade or otherwise, lent, hired out or otherwise circulated in any form of binding or cover other than that in which it is published. No part of this publication may be reproduced, stored in a retrieval system, or transmitted in any form or by any means (electronic, mechanical, photocopying, recording or otherwise) without prior written permission from the Author.

Scripture quotations: NKJV

A copy of this publication is legally deposited in The British Library.

ISBN: 978-1-0681515-6-9

www.marciampublishing.com

Dedication

For every individual who is experiencing life in all its glory. There's purpose in everything — just wait and see.

May you see the goodness of the Lord while you are here in the land of the living.
(Psalm 27:13)

Contents

Preface 7

How to navigate this book.. 8

Lesson 1: Get a hold of your mind first thing in the morning. 10

Lesson 2: Nine times out of ten it really isn't that serious. 12

Lesson 3: Every step you take is victory!... 14

Lesson 4: When we submit our will to God, it is surrendered, not extinguished. 16

Lesson 5: Have fun — live life!.. 18

Lesson 6: Don't let your experiences determine what you believe; let what you believe determine your experiences. 20

Lesson 7: Being comfortable in your own company is a sign of growth... 22

Lesson 8: Don't leave it until tomorrow. 24

Lesson 9: Sometimes you win, sometimes you learn. 26

Lesson 10: Don't just talk about it — do something about it. 28

Lesson 11: Never let your experiences with people determine your relationship with God... 30

Lesson 12: If we are not taking risks, we are not living a life of faith. 32

Lesson 13: Life is time, and time wasted cannot be recovered. 34

Lesson 14: Sometimes, purpose feels like disappointment. 36

Lesson 15: The fulfilment of our dreams will often test our character....... 38

Lesson 16: Prosperity is being in the will of God.................................. 40

Lesson 17: Have honest conversations with people you trust. 42

Lesson 18: Surround yourself with people who bring out the best in you. 44

Lesson 19: Anything that costs you your character is too expensive. 46

Lesson 20: Encouragers need encouraging too. 48

Lesson 21: Wake up every day and choose to be who God has called you to be. 50

Lesson 22: The quality of your life is a direct result of the choices you make. 52

Lesson 23: Jesus has done it all — everything! 54

Lesson 24: Strategically choose your thoughts. 56

Lesson 25: Rehearse what God says about you.. 58

Lesson 26: When something is true, you don't have to worry about defending it. 60

Lesson 27: Faith is the very foundation for us to reimagine our lives. 62

A lesson on identity 68

Imperfect Surrender 70

Acknowledgements 73

Preface

Writing is something I have always enjoyed. My 27th year was a challenging one and I decided to make note of 27 lessons I learnt throughout that year. I believe we are constantly learning throughout life, and this book is a compilation of the lessons that were most prominent during this part of my journey.

There is a part of me that embraces the now, while simultaneously looking toward the future. Ultimately, this is a book of hope. As you are reading, I hope that you find contentment with wherever you are at in life, while remaining hopeful that there are greater things you have yet to experience. You are not alone and I'm sure a lot of these lessons will be relatable. When you are finished, I hope that you feel encouraged to welcome the manifestation of an even better future, beyond what you are even able to imagine.

How to navigate this book

There are 27 lessons, each divided into three sections.

1. The lesson: this is the overall lesson.

2. The story behind the lesson: this is the background to what was happening in my life at the time I learnt this lesson.

3. The application of the lesson: this is possibly the most important section, because what's the use of learning without applying? This section highlights some ways in which the lesson can be applied to your life. The purpose of the application is to get you to reflect, take action, or even just to think about how you can live more abundantly.

You can read each lesson in chronological or non-chronological order — it's your choice.

At the end of Lesson 27, there are pages for you to take notes, and there is also a section for you to respond to the question, 'Which lesson/s do you relate to the most and why?'. Following this question, there is space for you to think about and make note of a couple of your own lessons and how you can apply them.

You might decide to read this book individually, or as a group, and use the lessons as points for discussion. This is a great opportunity for you to meet with a few trusted people to discuss what you've gained.

The final chapter is a spoken-word piece I wrote some years ago. It focuses on identity — an important part of life's journey.

Ready to learn? Let's go.

Sharee Benjamin-Robinson

LESSON 1

The lesson
Get a hold of your mind first thing in the morning.

The story behind the lesson
If you're anything like me, you either wake up singing, or thinking about whatever was on your mind the night before. I make a habit of reading a scripture and listening to something encouraging before I go to bed. It's my way of ending my day with positivity and peace. First thing in the morning, I say a simple prayer of thanks and a blessing over the day. The mind can be such a complex place. There's a passage in the Bible that encourages us to think about things that are true, noble, just, pure, lovely, and of good report. Basically, try to fill your mind with as much positivity as it can hold. Don't wait until something good happens during the day; you might have to wait too long for that. Make a conscious decision to focus on the good, first thing in the morning. As they say, start as you mean to go on.

The application of the lesson
Before you go to sleep tonight, read or listen to something you know will leave you thinking positive and peaceful thoughts. When you wake up, pronounce a blessing over the day, such as, "Today is a good day" or "Today is a blessed day". Tell your mind what kind of day it is.

LESSON 2

The Lesson
Nine times out of ten it really isn't that serious.

The story behind the lesson
If you're an overthinker like me, you've probably thought about a hundred different ways to resolve the same situation. It's tiring isn't it? When we take some time to think about it, we might find that it really isn't as serious as it first appeared. When we come to this realisation, it can save us from reacting in ways that are detrimental to the life we want to live. There are so many circumstances we have to experience in this life. There are things that are serious and we should approach them as such, and there are some things we know we can let go of (whether we want to, that's a different story). So, the next time you come across a difficult situation, take a moment to question the reality — is it really that serious?

The application of the lesson
Today, make a note of the things that have been on your mind. It may be one thing, or you may end up with a long list — the important thing is that you identify what has you in overthinking mode. Choose one thing from that list and decide whether it's as serious as it seemed when you first began to think about it. If it is, decide on the best way to approach it, if it isn't, replace it with a new, positive thought.

Sharee Benjamin-Robinson

LESSON 3

The Lesson
Every step you take is victory!

The story behind the lesson
In 2015, I travelled to South Africa, where I volunteered in a village for orphaned children. It was such an amazing experience. I felt like I'd come home to a place I'd never been to. It warms my heart whenever I think or talk about it. I was right where I needed to be. I had qualified as a teacher the year before and began to think about how I could pursue a career in international education, so I did my research and found two appropriate courses I could combine – I started my Master's degree in International Studies in Education and Development, which I successfully completed in 2019. One morning, as I walked along the paths of Birmingham University, I began to experience self-doubt; I was making my way to one of the more difficult modules and questioned whether I'd be able to make any contributions to the discussions. I was very aware of each step that was taking me closer and closer to the lecture room and, in a quest to encourage myself, these words came from my mouth – "Every step I take is victory!" I repeated the words over and over until I reached my destination. I don't recall how the class went that day, but the following year I put on my cap and gown and took some more victorious steps across the stage on graduation day. I made it!

The application of the lesson
Our awareness of the path we are on can become so intense the closer we get to our destination. It's almost as if our external world is overshadowed by our internal thought process. Are you moving towards completing a goal today? The important part is that you keep stepping in the right direction – the direction that will see you successfully reach the destination. Keep stepping, and with every step you take, whisper the word "victory".

Sharee Benjamin-Robinson

LESSON 4

The Lesson
When we submit our will to God, it is surrendered, not extinguished.

The story behind the lesson
Take a look around. I'll wait. Is life the way you wanted or expected it to be right now? One of my most prayed lines of prayer is, "Lord, let my will be in line with Your will." There are certain things I wanted from life that I thought I'd have by now, and I'm a great believer that I'd have them right now if God agreed with my timing. Let me be clear though: even though I believe, there have been times where I've felt as though my hope was fading and that God was withholding the good I've been asking for. However, I've found comfort in realising that God hasn't extinguished our desires — He simply says submit and surrender them. Our plans may be great, but when our will and God's will line up, now that's a life better than we can imagine.

The application of the lesson
Spend some time praying now. If you've never prayed before or you're not sure what to say, that's OK. Let's pray together.

"Lord, my life isn't the way I wanted or expected it to be, but today, I choose to trust You. Help me to submit and surrender my life plans to You, knowing that Your will for me is even greater than my own. I thank You that my life is in Your hands. Amen."

Sharee Benjamin-Robinson

LESSON 5

The Lesson
Have fun – live life!

The story behind the lesson
I've always been academic. I remember frequently turning down invitations during exam season and when assignments were due. When I first started teaching, I vowed that I wouldn't take any books home to mark – this was based on my teacher training experience. I was quite successful in keeping to this to begin with, but something else had to give. I would go into school earlier, stay late (literally until the caretaker told me to go home), do work on weekends and, when Monday came, I'd do it all again. As a result, whenever anyone would ask me to go out, my answer would quite frequently be, "I wish I could, but I've got too much work to do," followed by the face you make when you pretend to cry. Sad, right?

The application of the lesson
Now that I've experienced more of what life has to offer, I realise there's so much more to experience if I make time to embrace it. The world has taught us that we have to fit life around work. This often means we miss out on actually living. Don't feel guilty for making time to just have fun. Once yesterday has passed, it's gone forever. Have fun living a life you love, so when you think back to yesterday, instead of pretending to cry, you can genuinely smile.

Sharee Benjamin-Robinson

LESSON 6

The lesson
Don't let your experiences determine what you believe; let what you believe determine your experiences.

The story behind the lesson
Our system of belief may vary depending on what we are experiencing in life at the time. Everything is going to plan in our career, so we believe that as long as we work hard, we will reach our career goals. Nothing is going to plan in our career, so we believe that no matter how hard we work, things can, and eventually will, fail. This is what happens when we allow our experiences to determine what we believe about life — we become dependent on everything going well in order to have, and maintain, a positive outlook. Today, may you find it within yourself to believe that great things will happen to you. Ready for a new outlook?

The application of the lesson
Despite your experiences, let what you believe determine how you interpret them. Think about how you can approach the things that aren't going exactly to plan in your life right now, as well as the things that are. When you've found something that is achievable, add it to your daily to-do list, and see how things progress.

Sharee Benjamin-Robinson

LESSON 7

The Lesson

Being comfortable in your own company is a sign of growth.

The story behind the lesson

I love my own company. I enjoy the times when I can make the decision to just have some me-time. On the flip side though, there's been many a time when I've wanted to go somewhere or do something but haven't gone ahead with it because no one else wanted to — which of course meant that I'd have to ride solo. Consequently, I've missed out on a few experiences because I didn't want to do them alone. Relatable? When we get to a place where we begin to learn more about ourselves, and we begin that journey of self-discovery in a quest to find out who we are, we afford ourselves the opportunity to experience an abundant life. The one person we have to spend every day of our lives with is ourselves — it's going to be really tricky getting the best out of life if we aren't OK simply being in our company. May we all get to a place where we're so secure in our identity that, even if we have to go alone, we go anyway.

The application of the lesson

We all have something that we've been looking forward to doing but haven't done it yet. If you're ready, you don't have to wait for everyone else to be. As long as you're safe, whatever that something is for you today, schedule it in, put a date and time on it, and go for it. You are good company, you are good to be around, and you are taking steps to live abundantly as the person you are purposed to be. You've got this.

Sharee Benjamin-Robinson

LESSON 8

The Lesson
Don't leave it until tomorrow.

The story behind the lesson
Over the years, I have mastered the art of 'doing it tomorrow'. When we procrastinate, we postpone doing something knowing there will be consequences. Life can be very demanding and, as a result, sometimes the easy option is to leave our tasks until another time. I don't know about you, but if I need to do something for someone else, I'll get it done. If I need to do something for myself though, tomorrow often becomes two weeks, a month, a year, never. I've been working on this book since I was 27 years old but put it off for years. It's so easy to put ourselves on the back burner, but what benefit do we get from that?

The application of the lesson
Take a small step today. Think about one thing you've been putting off 'until tomorrow'. Allocate a part of your day to making a start on it. If it's something that takes time, try doing one thing that contributes to getting it done. Repeat this tomorrow and see how much you can accomplish.

Sharee Benjamin-Robinson

LESSON 9

The lesson
Sometimes you win, sometimes you learn.

The story behind the lesson
I live a life with no regrets. In doing so, I try not to see the loss in anything but rather, the lesson — what can I learn from this? A few years ago I decided to call off my engagement. I prayed, and I'd been going back and forth about my decision. One Sunday morning, it was as if I came to my senses, and in that moment, I knew it was time walk away. The winning would have looked like us walking up the aisle, but the learning was even greater than the win — I learnt so much about myself, about my strength, courage and wisdom, about how I deserved to be loved, and it helped me understand more of what I want and should expect from a godly man and a godly marriage. Yes, it's great when we win, but it's also great when we learn, because we often find that it changes the course of our lives. I've never been the same and I love the person I became. So, whether you're winning or learning, it's still win-win.

The application of the lesson
It's reflection time. Take a moment to reflect on a situation in your life that you chose to walk away from for the best. It's congratulations time. Congratulate and commend yourself for taking such a bold step, because we both know it wasn't easy. Now it's time to tell someone. Tell someone something positive that you've learnt about yourself. I'll always remember the feeling I had when I'd made my decision to leave — I felt a weight had been lifted off my shoulders, I felt freedom for the first time in a long time, and I cried tears of joy. I was, and am at peace.

Sharee Benjamin-Robinson

LESSON 10

The Lesson
Don't just talk about it — do something about it.

The story behind the lesson
Confession. I've been talking about 'doing something' with my writing for years. I've never been one to share my feelings, so I'd often write them down — in my diary, in a poem, in the notes on my phone, and so on. The first time I shared one of my poems, I was 12 years old. The feedback I got was beyond what I expected. I don't even know what I expected, but it ignited something in me that said I needed to share more of what I'd written. And really, I was writing about life. I was just writing from a place of experience, whether it was my own, or the experiences I'd witnessed of others, and it was reaching people in a way I hadn't anticipated. For years people had told me to write a book and for years my response has been, "Yeah, I will." The reality of it is this: I was saying it outwardly, but inwardly I didn't believe I could. I didn't think people would understand where I was coming from, so I continued to just talk about it as the years went by. Until now.

The application of the lesson
People who are gifted at encouraging others often find it hard to take their own advice. Guilty. What have you been talking about doing? Be open and receptive to encouragement from others. People need to hear you. Don't just talk about it. Today, do something about it.

Sharee Benjamin-Robinson

LESSON 11

The lesson
Never let your experiences with people determine your relationship with God.

The story behind the lesson
For anyone who has grown up in church, you may be familiar with a little experience called 'church hurt'. For the most part, being a part of a church family is a beautiful experience; not only do we develop our relationship with God, but we are loved and involved in fellowship with one another. It's a home from home. Plot twist. I had one particular experience that caused me to lose trust in the very people I thought would uphold me. I was disheartened. I was disappointed. And yet, it was the closest I'd ever felt to God. I understand why people step away from faith. Yes, the Christian journey is about us following Christ, but on this journey, we need people. But people fail, people let us down, people cause harm. Our experiences with people are unpredictable no matter who they are, but one thing remains: God is always faithful.

The application of the lesson
Is there anyone whom you are allowing to determine your relationship with God? People won't always realise they've hurt you, even when you've addressed it with them. Today, ask God to direct you in how you should deal with the experience. Ask God to heal you, because healing isn't just for physical ailments; some of us need healing emotionally. The journey is personal. I pray that no matter what the outcome, your relationship with God grows stronger.

Sharee Benjamin-Robinson

LESSON 12

The Lesson
If we are not taking risks, we are not living a life of faith.

The story behind the lesson
I love a good devotional. I'd begun a new one and on this particular day, the writer was addressing the topic of 'courage'. Within this, they spoke about risks. Then it dawned on me: the 'faith' that we have is what most people would call 'risk-taking'. Let's address faith for a moment. The biblical definition is, 'the substance of things hoped for, the evidence of things not seen' (Hebrews 11:1). We see here that faith and hope are interlinked. Faith is the substance of hope, and we hope for things we cannot already see, but because faith is the evidence, it enables us to see the things we are hoping for; so really, through faith, we can see what we can't see (read that again; I know it was a lot to take in). So this is it — even though we experience uncertainties, we actively live a life of faith when we choose to pursue the things we hope for.

The application of the lesson
When we take a risk, we dare to do the things that might not work out — this is faith lived out. Think of something you've been seeing as "too risky". Now turn that around and think of it as something that requires faith. Do you feel differently about it now? Whatever your answer is, make a choice today — choose faith.

Sharee Benjamin-Robinson

LESSON 13

The lesson
Life is time, and time wasted cannot be recovered.

The story behind the lesson
I was at a funeral. The speaker was sharing words of encouragement for family and friends and this line made so much sense: every second that passes is gone forever. There is no way to reclaim it. No way of actually reliving the moment. Recovery is not possible. When time is gone, it's gone. Indefinitely. It was too late for the person who had passed away, so this message was for those of us who sat inaudibly, shoulder to shoulder in pews facing the coffin. It really hit home — for me personally anyway.

The application of the lesson
We all waste time at some point in our lives. Procrastination is a thief, and even though we know this, I'm sure there have been multiple occasions where the label 'time-waster' would be a befitting description of our status. We're human, and this means that life will come to an end. Although we cannot recover time, we can redeem it. The fact that we are alive means we can make the most of the time we have now. So from now on, redeem the time.

Sharee Benjamin-Robinson

LESSON 14

The lesson
Sometimes, purpose feels like disappointment.

The story behind the lesson
To live our purpose sometimes means to experience disappointment. There are times when life simply doesn't make sense; we experience uncertainty and it feels as though we are misaligned. We feel disappointed because things didn't work out how we wanted them to, but the reality of it is this: sometimes, for us to live in our purpose, things can't go the way we want them to. Living in purpose isn't always a narrow road; at times, the road is broad and we don't know which route to take, and yet, there is always a way to get back on track.

The application of the lesson
The fact that you are alive in this very moment is a testament to the fact that you still have purpose in this life. What does it mean to have purpose? Use this question as a starting point to discovering what impact you are meant to have on this world. You might be in a place where you feel disappointed, but today, seek clarity on your purpose. There's still time.

Sharee Benjamin-Robinson

LESSON 15

The Lesson
The fulfilment of our dreams will often test our character.

The story behind the lesson
Have you ever felt tested? Not like an exam type of test (at least we get to prepare for those) — I mean a test that you didn't see coming, that you didn't expect. For our dreams to be fulfilled: the strength of our character, the authenticity of our character, and the stability of our character, will be tested. To date, a lot of my dreams have been fulfilled. These are mostly the ones I have control over — gaining my degrees and buying my home, for example. There are some dreams I am waiting to see manifested in my life. Some of these dreams require a lot more preparation and trust. I've found that these are the ones that have tested me the most. These are the dreams that require us to hold on to the integrity of our character. The wait will be worth it.

The application of the lesson
What can you do to contribute to the dreams you are waiting to be fulfilled? Do what you can do, and leave the rest in God's hands.

Sharee Benjamin-Robinson

LESSON 16

The Lesson
Prosperity is being in the will of God.

The story behind the lesson
Let's put that into an equation, prosperity = being in God's will. I mentioned this point in Lesson 4 and I find the need to mention it again. One of my most prayed lines of prayer is, "Lord, let my will be in line with Your will." To be prosperous is to be in the will of God. At the start of a new year, I tend to pray for a year of peace, love, and prosperity. Peace often comes fairly frequently, give or take a few 'under-the-weather' seasons. Love comes in its various forms, but prosperity seems to be the most complex of the three. It's often linked to accomplishing goals, becoming wealthy, being successful in certain areas of life, that sort of thing — I find that it's slightly more difficult to evidence. One thing I've learnt is that being in the will of God is equal to being prosperous; we may not have achieved prosperity in the eyes of others, or even in our own eyes, but being aligned with God's will is what it truly means to be prosperous.

The application of the lesson
It's a really simple application — join me in praying one of my most prayed prayers: "Lord, let my will be in line with Your will. Amen."

Sharee Benjamin-Robinson

LESSON 17

The Lesson
Have honest conversations with people you trust.

The story behind the lesson
Some friends and I went on a girls' trip one Easter. On this particular day, we got back from our excursions and decided we would have a chilled evening. We put on the T-shirts we'd got from our outing the day before and gathered in one room. It was totally unplanned, but we had the most honest conversations we'd ever had with each other. The people we can open up to may change depending on our experiences with them and the season of our life. We can't talk to everyone because, let's be real, not everyone has our best interests at heart. But we really need people we can be honest with. Got some people?

The application of the lesson
If you're anything like me, you love your own space. It's necessary to have people in our lives we can share our space with though — family or friends we know we can have those real-talk conversations with. It's not too late to start building those connections if they don't already exist, and if they do, do all that you can to ensure the trust remains strong.

Sharee Benjamin-Robinson

LESSON 18

The lesson
Surround yourself with people who bring out the best in you.

The story behind the lesson
Let me be very honest with this. Some people drain my energy and disturb my peace. I'm sure you understand what I mean, right? I try my best to choose my company wisely. There are some people I choose to spend my time with, and there are some whose presence I avoid — on purpose. This isn't mean — it's necessary. People who bring out the best in you are a blessing, and it works both ways. Sharing their company feels good. Part of living a fulfilled life is having people to share it with. So choose those people wisely. It'll make all the difference.

The application of the lesson
I hope that there's at least one person in your life who makes your light shine brighter. If there's someone who comes to mind, arrange to meet with them, thank them, and enjoy each other's company.

Sharee Benjamin-Robinson

LESSON 19

The Lesson
Anything that costs you your character is too expensive.

The story behind the lesson
Have you ever played a whole scenario in your head but not actually acted it out in real-time? Yes? Well it was probably for the best. Some situations do require us to voice our thoughts and, for other situations, we need to take a moment to consider the consequences. I believe that our character is constantly being developed. It's dependent on our life experiences, our environment, and even our thought processes. But one thing I've observed is that once a person's character has been tarnished, it's quite difficult to retrieve. It's a high price to pay — too high in fact.

The application of the lesson
If you've been confronted with a situation that needs to be dealt with, take a moment to think about how you can respond to it in a way that addresses the situation, while also keeping your good character intact.

Sharee Benjamin-Robinson

LESSON 20

The lesson
Encouragers need encouraging too.

The story behind the lesson
One thing about me is, I'll encourage someone all day and then find it hard to take on my own advice (I literally just rolled my eyes at myself). In my opinion, people who are generally good at encouraging others, often find it difficult to share their personal feelings, and so, in a quest to keep their feelings hidden, they present an "I'm OK" exterior (it's my opinion, but I'm also speaking from a place of experience). People often see a person's strength and resilience and take this to mean that person is always OK. This is very seldom the case. Encouragers need to be encouraged.

The application of the lesson
Is there someone you know to be an encourager? Send them that 'just checking in' message they so frequently send to you and others. See how they're feeling, and even if they're doing well, use it as an opportunity to encourage them. Trust me, they'll be so thankful for it.

Maybe you're the encourager. First of all, thank you. I'll assume that you give good, sound advice. Write down some of the positive advice you've given to others that you know has been received well. Read it aloud, encourage yourself, and apply it. You may need to hear some encouraging words from someone else, maybe pray that God would send someone to encourage you today.

Sharee Benjamin-Robinson

LESSON 21

The Lesson
Wake up every day and choose to be who God has called you to be.

The story behind the lesson
God has spoken many beautiful things over us — "But you *are* a chosen generation, a royal priesthood, a holy nation, His own special people" (1 Peter 2:9), "For we are His workmanship" (Ephesians 2:10). The reality is though, we don't always accept or believe these things. What do we do then? I've heard these wonderful words time and time again since childhood. There are times when I can say them with confidence, and there are times when my reality is just not conducive to this level of positive vibes. This is why it has to be a choice. As human beings, we have the potential to be in a constant battle with our mind. One day we're feeling so worthy of all the greatness life has to offer, and the next we're unsure what relevance these scriptures have in the context of our reality. But we must choose to behold the authenticity of who God has called us to be.

The application of the lesson
Make a note of the scriptures above and any others that remind you of the good things that have been written and spoken over your life. Once you've done this, share them with someone or even a group. Now, be accountable to one another. Whenever any of you are feeling unworthy, send out a reminder of these, and choose to believe.

Sharee Benjamin-Robinson

LESSON 22

The lesson
The quality of your life is a direct result of the choices you make.

The story behind the lesson
I was watching a movie one evening; it was a random one I came across but it had a good message. The main character was a female who was living an unfulfilled life. As if by chance, she stumbles across a former classmate, and following their encounter, she wishes she could redo life in a quest to change everything. Her wish is granted. Her quality of life improved significantly because of the changes she made when given another chance. Now, we can't change the past, but we can ensure that our today and our future is one of good quality. The daily choices we make affect the quality of our life and often the lives of those around us. What kind of life do you desire?

The application of the lesson
There might be a part of your life that you desire to change. Start today. Make a note of whatever it is and list some of the ways in which you can ensure a better future for yourself and those around you. Once you're done, read this scripture from Psalm 37 verses 4-5: "Delight yourself also in the Lord, and He shall give you the desires of your heart. Commit your way to the Lord, trust also in Him, and He shall bring it to pass." Amen.

Sharee Benjamin-Robinson

LESSON 23

The Lesson

Jesus has done it all — everything!

The story behind the lesson

Imagine. Within one sacrifice, everything we would ever need was taken care of. Literally everything. I don't even know if it's possible to truly comprehend this, and with the reality of life, sometimes it definitely doesn't feel like all our needs have been met, whether personally or even in the world around us. Whatever your need is today, come to Jesus, trust and believe that He has dealt with it, and await the manifestation. It is done.

The application of the lesson

Write down your needs, even the ones that seem small. Now, say a prayer of thanksgiving that Jesus has already met those needs. All you have to do now is await the manifestation. Remember to revisit your notes when these things come to pass and say another thanksgiving prayer.

Sharee Benjamin-Robinson

LESSON 24

The lesson
Strategically choose your thoughts.

The story behind the lesson
I have the tendency to overthink. I've probably mentioned this already, and if I haven't, I probably will. I know for a fact this is a relatable trait, and being as there are few things we can control, I'm not sure why overthinking is such a prominent feature in our lives. If you're an overthinker, choosing your thoughts wisely is essential — I would even go as far to say that it's compulsory. Many things are out of our control, but one thing we have control over is our thoughts. I mentioned a verse in the Bible that encourages us to think about what is good and worthy of praise, things that are true, honourable, right, pure, beautiful, and respected. What's significant about this verse is that it was written by a man named Paul who, at the time of writing, was in prison. He could have chosen to think about all the negatives associated with his situation, but he strategically chose thoughts of optimism. If we must overthink, may we think over and over again about these things. We can't control everything, but peace comes when we believe in the sovereignty of our Creator. If we are strategic with the thoughts we choose, we can change the trajectory of our whole life. Ready for some changes?

The application of the lesson
Let's start those changes right now. Think of the things that are good, worthy of praise, true, honourable, right, pure, beautiful, and respected — maybe focus on one at a time over the next few days. Whenever your thoughts try to run away with you, bring yourself back to the centre and focus on these things.

Sharee Benjamin-Robinson

LESSON 25

The lesson
Rehearse what God says about you.

The story behind the lesson
I wrote a spoken-word piece some years ago entitled, 'Imperfect Surrender' — which you can read at the end of this book. It's all about coming into an acceptance of how great we are. Once rehearsals have taken place, an individual is then expected to know whatever they have been learning off by heart; it may be lines for a play, a song, a piece of music, or in this case, the Word of God. God wants us to know who we are in Him; this is where we find our true identity.

The application of the lesson
Grab a pen and paper, open the notes on your phone, turn to the notes pages in this book, whatever you choose — it's time to jot some things down. Now open your Bible or Bible app or even have a conversation with someone. Write down at least seven scripture verses (one for each day of the week) that tell you about the great person God has made you. The point of a rehearsal is to practise the delivery of a performance. Every day, rehearse these verses. And when I say rehearse, I mean take it to the stage and imagine you are about to perform these words in front of the masses. Create your own stage. Ready? Action.

Sharee Benjamin-Robinson

LESSON 26

The lesson
When something is true, you don't have to worry about defending it.

The story behind the lesson
"What if people think…?" I'm sure many of us have begun a sentence with these four words. It's not so much of a hindrance now, but there was a period in my life where I was overly concerned with how people perceived me. This didn't help the overthinking, and over the years, I've learnt that people will always think what they want to think, and what matters most is the truth. When you have confidence in your character, you don't have to be concerned about how others may or may not interpret your choices. There are times when the truth requires an explanation, but it doesn't need a defender. When the truth is the truth, you can let it speak for itself.

The application of the lesson
Let the truth speak for itself. It's as simple as that.

Sharee Benjamin-Robinson

LESSON 27

The lesson
Faith is the very foundation for us to reimagine our lives.

The story behind the lesson
Hands up if you're a daydreamer. I imagine a number of hands shooting up with the words, "Yep, that's me all day," and a few more tentative hands reaching up halfway as you pondered whether you daydream or just zone out frequently. Either way, in those moments, I often think of things I'm hoping for. I literally narrate a whole storyline with scenes to go with it. Faith and hope are interconnected. I often find myself reimagining life, and it's so beautiful. What's even more beautiful is that, by faith, our thoughts can become our reality.

The application of the lesson
What beautiful things are you hoping will happen in your life? Think about them, write them down, or share them with someone. By faith (the substance of things hoped for, the evidence of things not seen), see these things as a reality in your life. What a beautiful scene.

Which lesson/s do you relate to the most and why?

Your turn! Write down three lessons you've learnt this year and think of ways you can apply them.

A lesson I've learnt this year

How will I apply it to my life?

A lesson I've learnt this year

How will I apply it to my life?

A lesson I've learnt this year

How will I apply it to my life?

Notes

A lesson on identity

I hope that you have experienced a journey of self-discovery throughout this book. We are constantly living and, as a result of that, we are constantly learning. We are living and learning simultaneously. As we do so, we are coming into identity. I also write poetry/spoken word and want to share one of my spoken word pieces with you. It expresses how, when we surrender our lives to Christ, there may still be parts of us that we hold on to. When we make a decision to receive salvation, we give our all over to God, but in our human nature, what frequently occurs is that we only give part of ourselves, which is what makes our surrender, imperfect. That is how the title, 'Imperfect Surrender', came about.

In terms of the content, there are various elements to it. This piece speaks of how the imperfections that we have do not faze God. I begin by writing the words, "He delights in my imperfections," ('He' being God) and the reason I feel this way is because, if we are already perfect, then there is no requirement for change. I then go on to address some of the factors that contribute to us being imperfectly surrendered. These are the things that cause us to bypass and neglect the opportunities we have to be like the people we often admire in scripture. They prevent us from living the life of abundance we have been promised in Christ. There are also ways in which we are so acquainted with the Word of God: we read it, we study it, we hear the word preached, but we don't receive it for ourselves, we don't accept the promises God has spoken over our lives. In order for us to come into alignment, we need to surrender the things that cause us to feel insecure, that cause us to feel inadequate and unworthy. We have to be freed from these in order to make room for the promises of God to be fulfilled in our lives. We can then live in our true identity. We can be changed.

Imperfect Surrender

He delights in my imperfections because it means He has something to work with.

The work to be done extends much further than this, but the mere fact that I allow the insecurity of my being to force me into the security of being satisfied with less, it concerns Him.

Insecurity. A state subject to uncertainty or anxiety, maybe not physically but a vessel that is open to embody the characteristics of one who really doesn't know their worth.

Rather stay bound by the insecurities of life because it's familiar territory, giving up the opportunity to receive the abundant blessing of boldness as given unto Esther, the power and authority to lead like Nehemiah and the confident trust shown in the obedience of Mary, nope...not me, or so insecurity would force me to believe.

Had the ability to believe in everyone but me, always did see the potential in others but when reflecting on oneself, maybe not clear to others but clear to me all I could see was insecurity.

I knew it wasn't how He intended for me to be, but I didn't know how to escape the trap. It was learnt behaviour and I had become so attached.

I was well acquainted with the Word, "you are fearfully and wonderfully made", "you are a royal priesthood a holy nation", "you are an heir and co-heirs with Christ."

The mind made it so hard to accept and when faced with reality of life it seemed like the Word just didn't apply.

So what next?

I had to provide a vacancy for courage and self-esteem, every part of my being had been allocated so it was time to get pen and paper and administer redundancy: fear, anxiety, doubt, worthlessness, comparison, affliction, temptation, frustration, lack of confidence, your contract has ended.

Love, joy, peace, patience, kindness, goodness, faithfulness, gentleness, self-control, boldness, strength, courage and wisdom, I am your new occupation.

I am accepted

I am a child of the King of kings

I am complete in Christ

I am no longer bound or condemned

I am free

I am a conqueror; no, I am more than a conqueror

I am an overcomer, my Saviour has overcome the world

I am a believer in a God who is faithful to complete the good work He started in me

I am born of God and no evil can harm me

I am significant

I am secure

I have been chosen and appointed to bear fruit

I am God's workmanship

I can do all things through Christ who strengthens me

I surrendered all to You and only then was I able to accept Your Word.

No longer possessing the state of vulnerability to uncertainty and anxiety but You gave me the ability to cast down burdens and openly invite Your Spirit. So, if any be looking for You let them find You in me, may I be your reflection, a new creation.

I... am... changed!

Sharee Benjamin-Robinson

Acknowledgements

I praise God daily for His faithfulness and His promises. For the times He reminded me that He would be faithful to complete the good work He started in me.

I would like to thank my parents and family, who have supported me through all of these lessons (and the rest). To my wonderful Mom, my constant, my prayer warrior, my fashion icon, the first (and for a while, the only) person I told about my intention to finally put my writing into book form. Your love has been tangible since forever. Thank you for the countless number of times you asked, "Shaz, aren't you writing your book?" It encouraged me so much to keep pursuing my goal. Dad aka Mr Rob, my quiet prayer, my music partner, and personal legal advisor, I remember the period of my life that drew us closer. Thank you for your love and support; I appreciate it more than you probably know. I'm honestly so grateful for my parents – you are my blessings. I love you both a lot.

To my grandmothers, whom I miss dearly, I'm blessed to have loved and been loved by you both (my adopted Grandmothers included), and I know you'd both say something like, "My granddaughter wrote a book, you know" (but the patois version).

I'm thankful for the people who remain steadfast, my genuine friends who became family – you know who you are.

I would like to pay special acknowledgement to Benjamin Zephaniah. Even as you rest, I'm thankful for your encouragement, always.

To Marcia and the team at Marcia M Publishing, thank you for your work behind the scenes and for seeing this accomplishment through with me.

I'm generally not a crier, but I feel myself tearing up as I write these acknowledgements because they are testaments of how blessed I am to have people to thank. So whether you call me Sharee, Shaz, Sharisha Rob, Shez, Ree, Ree Ree, Shug, Sher, the list goes on… I thank you. To you, the reader, you may not know me personally, you had no obligation to purchase or read my book and yet, look at you, here supporting me as well. I'm thankful to you too.

Finally, to my 27th year. You taught me that all life's lessons contribute to the woman I am. You made me realise — in the words of India Arie — that strength, courage, and wisdom has been inside of me all along.

God bless you all.

Shaz x

www.marciampublishing.com

www.ingramcontent.com/pod-product-compliance
Lightning Source LLC
Chambersburg PA
CBHW052115070526
44584CB00017B/2500